GRAPHIC AMERICA

The REVOLUTION IN INDUSTRY

JOHN PERRITANO

Crabtree Publishing Company
www.crabtreebooks.com

Crabtree Publishing Company
www.crabtreebooks.com

Author:
John Perritano
Coordinating editor:
Chester Fisher
Editors:
Scholastic Ventures Inc.
Molly Aloian
Copy editor:
Scholastic Ventures Inc.
Proofreaders:
Adrianna Morganelli
Crystal Sikkens
Project editor:
Robert Walker
Print and production coordinator:
Katherine Berti
Prepress technician:
Ken Wright
Logo design:
Samantha Crabtree
Project manager:
Santosh Vasudevan (Q2AMedia)
Art direction:
Rahul Dhiman (Q2AMedia)
Design:
Tarang Saggar (Q2AMedia)
Illustrations:
Q2AMedia

Library and Archives Canada Cataloguing in Publication

Perritano, John
The revolution in industry / John Perritano.

(Graphic America)
Includes index.
ISBN 978-0-7787-4189-3 (bound).--ISBN 978-0-7787-4216-6 (pbk.)

1. Technological innovations--Comic books, strips, etc.--Juvenile literature. 2. Industrialization--Comic books, strips, etc.--Juvenile literature. I. Title. II. Series.

T173.8.P47 2008 j609 C2008-906283-3

Library of Congress Cataloging-in-Publication Data

Perritano, John.
The revolution in industry / John Perritano.
p. cm. -- (Graphic America)
Includes index.
ISBN-13: 978-0-7787-4216-6 (pbk. : alk. paper)
ISBN-10: 0-7787-4216-4 (pbk. : alk. paper)
ISBN-13: 978-0-7787-4189-3 (reinforced library binding : alk. paper)
ISBN-10: 0-7787-4189-3 (reinforced library binding : alk. paper)
1. Technological innovations--Juvenile literature. 2. Industrialization--Juvenile literature. I. Title. II. Series.

T173.8.K47 1990
609--dc22

2008041855

Crabtree Publishing Company Printed in Canada/052020/CPC20200512
www.crabtreebooks.com 1-800-387-7650

In Canada: We acknowledge the financial support of the Government of Canada through the Canada Book Fund for our publishing activities.

Published in Canada
Crabtree Publishing
616 Welland Ave.
St. Catharines, ON
L2M 5V6

Published in the United States
Crabtree Publishing
PMB 59051
350 Fifth Avenue, 59th Floor
New York, New York 10118

Published in the United Kingdom
Crabtree Publishing
Maritime House
Basin Road North, Hove
BN41 1WR

Published in Australia
Crabtree Publishing
3 Charles Street
Coburg North
VIC, 3058

CONTENTS

QUEST FOR POWER

THEY HAVE ALSO BUILT SUBMARINES THAT GET THEIR ENERGY FROM NUCLEAR POWER...

AND SPACE STATIONS POWERED BY ENERGY FROM THE SUN.

PEOPLE POWER

ANIMAL POWER

WIND POWER

THE WIND PROVIDED LOTS OF POWER, TOO. EARLY **IMMIGRANTS** TO AMERICA FROM THE NETHERLANDS BUILT WINDMILLS TO GRIND GRAIN.

WIND MOVED MIGHTY SHIPS ACROSS VAST OCEANS.

WATER POWER

RUSHING WATER TURNED SAW BLADES THAT CUT TREES INTO BOARDS.

WATER ALSO POWERED CARTING MILLS THAT TURNED FLEECE INTO THREAD.

THE STEAM ENGINE

AS THE YEARS PASSED, PEOPLE TRIED TO DISCOVER BETTER WAYS TO MAKE POWER. IN 1690, FRENCH SCIENTIST DENIS PAPIN INVENTED A SIMPLE STEAM ENGINE. IN 1769, JAMES WATT A SCOTTISH INVENTOR, **PATENTED** THE FIRST MODERN STEAM ENGINE. THE REVOLUTION IN POWER HAD BEGUN.

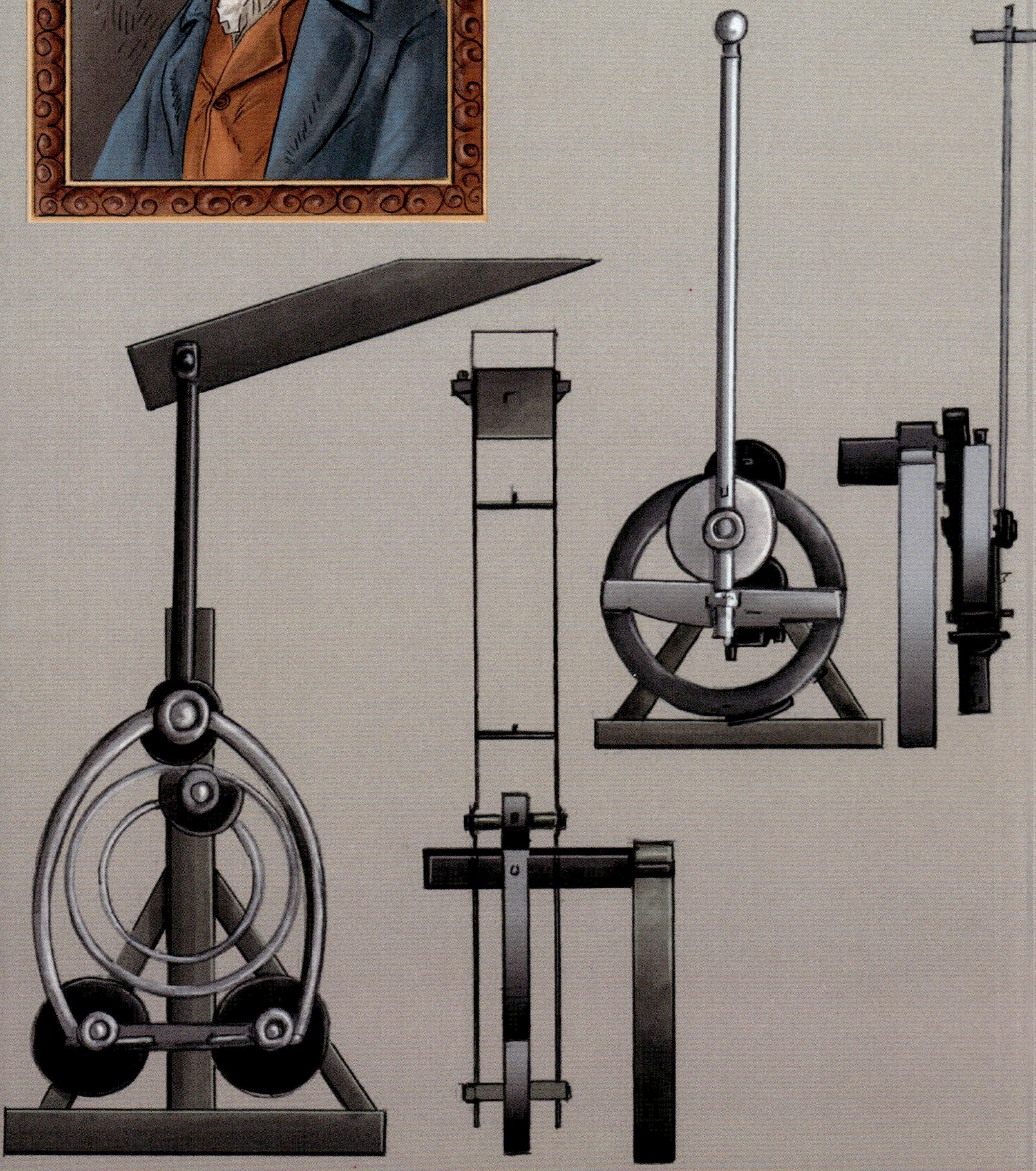

THE STEAM ENGINE COMPLETELY CHANGED SOCIETY. THE ENGINE USED THE **POTENTIAL ENERGY** OF STEAM. IT CHANGED THIS INTO **MECHANICAL ENERGY**. OTHER INVENTORS DISCOVERED DIFFERENT WAYS TO USE THE ENGINE. IN 1783, MARQUIS CLAUDE FRANCOIS DE JOUFFROY D'ABBANS LAUNCHED THE FIRST STEAMBOAT DOWN THE SEINE RIVER IN FRANCE.
I'D SURE LIKE TO GET ABOARD THAT BEAUTY.
WE COULD GO TO NEW YORK CITY, LICKITY-SPLIT.
ON AUGUST 22, 1787, JOHN FITCH LAUNCHED THE FIRST AMERICAN STEAMBOAT. IN 1807, ROBERT FULTON'S STEAMBOAT, CLERMONT, MADE A FIVE-HOUR TRIP FROM NEW YORK CITY UP THE HUDSON RIVER TO ALBANY.

STEAM TRAINS

MR. MCCREEDY, WHERE ARE YOU GOING TO TODAY?
TAKIN' THE OLE' JOHN BULL TO PERTH AMBOY, SON. SEE YA IN A COUPLE OF DAYS.
IT WAS NOT LONG BEFORE STEAM TRAINS STARTED MOVING BOTH **FREIGHT** AND PEOPLE. TOWNS QUICKLY GREW ALONG RAILROAD STOPS. THE RAILROAD COMPANIES CREATED THOUSANDS OF JOBS. BUSINESSES IN TOWNS ALONG A TRAIN'S ROUTE NEEDED WORKERS. THE RAILROAD NEEDED PEOPLE TO MOVE FREIGHT ON AND OFF TRAINS. FACTORIES HIRED MORE WORKERS TO HELP MEET THE DEMAND WHEN ITEMS SOLD AROUND THE COUNTRY.

THEY SAY THOSE IRON HORSES CAN MOVE TONS OF SUPPLIES FROM CHICAGO CLEAR TO SAN FRANCISCO IN FOUR DAYS.
NOTHIN' CAN MOVE THAT FAST.
BY THE LATE 1800S, STEAM TRAINS BECAME SO IMPORTANT THAT A RAILROAD WAS BUILT CONNECTING THE EAST COAST OF THE UNITED STATES TO THE WEST COAST. THE RAILROAD CUT TRAVEL TIME FROM SIX MONTHS TO SIX DAYS. COULD ANYTHING TOP THE STEAM ENGINE?

THE INTERNAL COMBUSTION ENGINE

GOTTLIEB DAIMLER IS A VERY INVENTIVE FELLOW, DON'T YOU THINK EVA?
I'M AFRAID HE'S GOING TO GET HURT RIDING THAT THING.
IN 1885, GOTTLIEB DAIMLER TOOK OTTO'S ENGINE AND PUT IT ON A WOODEN-FRAMED BICYCLE THAT HE CALLED THE "BONE CRUSHER." DAIMLER HAD JUST BUILT THE FIRST MOTORCYCLE.

THE AUTOMOBILE

ALMOST OVERNIGHT, DOZENS OF COMPANIES STARTED BUILDING AUTOMOBILES. EACH MOTORCAR WAS BUILT BY HAND AND VERY EXPENSIVE. HENRY FORD CHANGED ALL THAT WHEN HE BEGAN TO BUILD A HUGE NUMBER OF CARS ON AN **ASSEMBLY LINE**.

FORD'S ASSEMBLY LINE CUT THE TIME IT TOOK TO BUILD A CAR FROM 12 1/2 HOURS TO SIX HOURS. FORD'S MODEL TS WERE NO-FRILL AUTOS. THEY ALL LOOKED ALIKE AND ONLY CAME IN ONE COLOR—BLACK. FORD SOLD MILLIONS OF THEM.
CHARLIE, WATCH OUT, YOU'RE GOING TO KILL US!

THE WRIGHT STUFF

THE INTERNAL COMBUSTION ENGINE IMPACTED PEOPLE'S LIVES IN MANY WAYS. YET, IT TOOK TWO BROTHERS FROM DAYTON, OHIO—ORVILLE AND WILBUR WRIGHT—TO TAKE THE ENGINE TO NEW HEIGHTS. THEY USED IT TO BUILD THE FIRST MECHANICALLY POWERED AIRPLANE.

DECEMBER 17, 1903, WAS A COOL AND WINDY DAY ON THE REMOTE ISLAND OF KITTY HAWK, NORTH CAROLINA. AT 10:35 A.M., ORVILLE WRIGHT CLIMBED ABOARD A STRANGE-LOOKING MACHINE WITH WINGS. THE GASOLINE-POWERED ENGINE TURNED THE MACHINE'S TWO PROPELLERS.

WITH THE PROPELLERS SPINNING AND WILBUR RUNNING ALONG SIDE, THE MACHINE WENT DOWN A WOODEN RAIL AT SEVEN MILES (11 KM) PER HOUR. AS THE AIRPLANE LUMBERED ALONG THE SKIDS, IT BEGAN TO RISE SLOWLY.

ONLY MOMENTS LATER, THE AIRPLANE ROSE TO A HEIGHT OF ABOUT 10 FEET (THREE METERS). IT FLEW FOR AN AMAZING 120 FEET (37 M). ORVILLE WRIGHT HAD BECOME THE FIRST PERSON TO FLY A MOTORIZED AIRCRAFT.

SOARING HIGHER

THE WRIGHT BROTHERS' FLIGHT LASTED ONLY 12 SECONDS, BUT IT CHANGED THE WORLD. ***ENGINEERS*** *SOON MADE THE WRIGHT BROTHERS' INVENTION SLEEKER, FASTER, AND LARGER. THIS AMAZING INVENTION WAS FIRST USED DURING WORLD WAR I (1914-1918). FRANCE, GERMANY, GREAT BRITAIN, AND THE UNITED STATES USED THE AIRPLANES AS A WEAPON FOR THE FIRST TIME. GUNS WERE MOUNTED ON AIRPLANES, AND FIGHTING TOOK TO THE SKIES.*

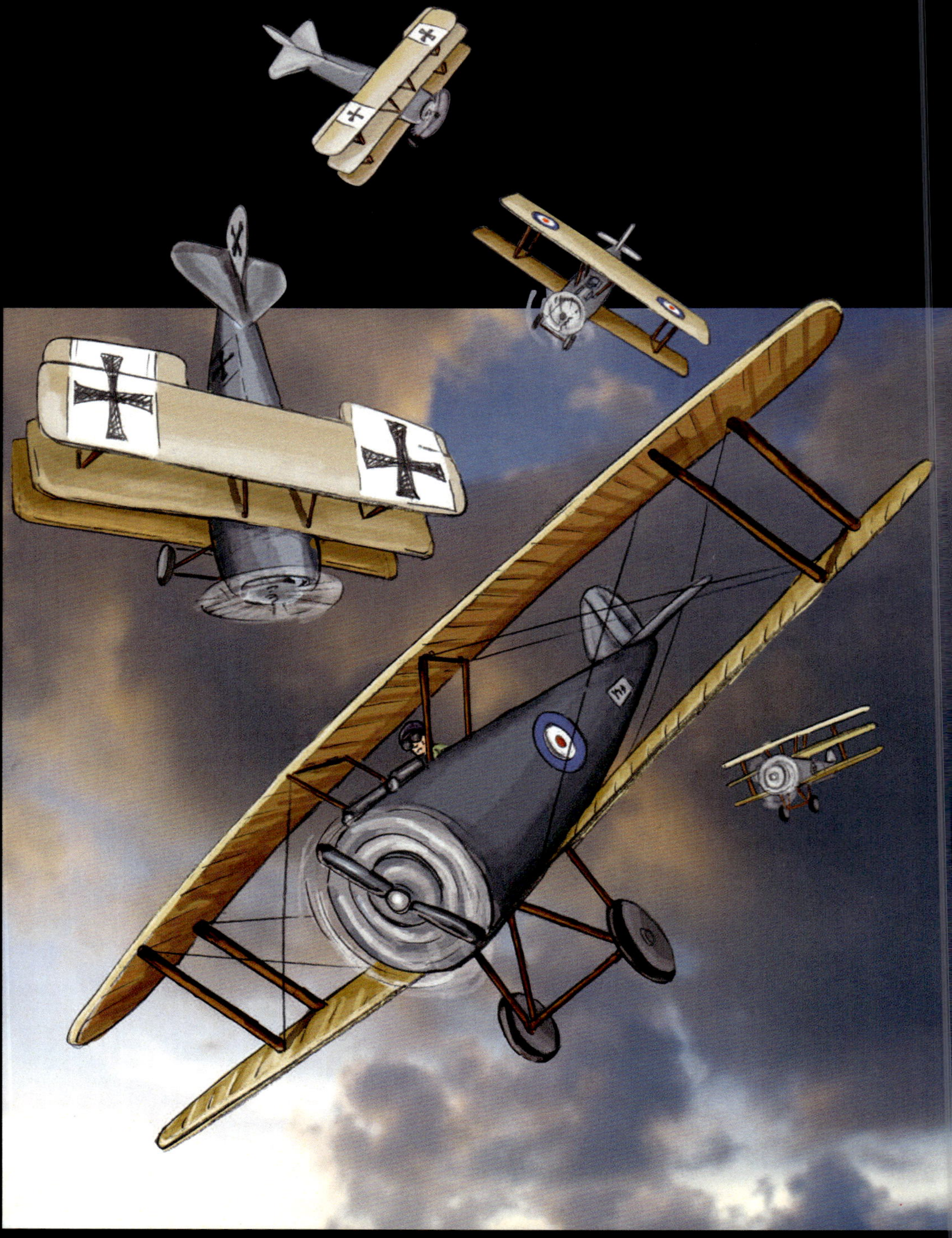

*PROPELLER AIRPLANES GAVE WAY TO THE **JET** BY THE 1940S. JET ENGINES MADE AIRPLANES FLY FASTER THAN THE SPEED OF SOUND, ABOUT 700 MILES (1127 KM) AN HOUR. CAPTAIN CHARLES "CHUCK" YEAGER WAS THE FIRST TO BREAK THE SOUND BARRIER ON OCTOBER 14, 1947, IN A JET HE NAMED AFTER HIS WIFE.*

ROCKETS AND MORE

BY THE 1950S, ROCKET ENGINES PROVIDED ENOUGH POWER FOR PEOPLE TO ESCAPE EARTH'S GRAVITY. THE SATURN V ROCKET, WHICH SENT PEOPLE TO THE MOON, WAS THE MOST POWERFUL ROCKET EVER BUILT.

THE MAIN ENGINES OF THE SPACE SHUTTLE USE LIQUID HYDROGEN AND OXYGEN AS FUEL. THE ENGINES PROVIDE ENOUGH POWER FOR THE SHUTTLE TO SPEED UP FROM 3,000 MILES PER HOUR (4,828 KM/H) TO 17,000 MILES PER HOUR (27,359 KM/H) IN JUST SIX MINUTES.
USA

NUCLEAR POWER

*NO POWER IS AS GREAT AS THE ENERGY CREATED BY A **NUCLEAR REACTION**. SCIENTISTS DISCOVERED THE POWER OF THE ATOM IN 1945. SCIENTISTS UNDERSTOOD THAT IF THEY COULD BREAK APART JUST ONE SMALL ATOM, THE REACTION WOULD RELEASE A GREAT AMOUNT OF ENERGY. THEY SPLIT URANIUM ATOMS TO CREATE A VERY STRONG SOURCE OF POWER.*

SCIENTISTS LEARNED HOW TO CONTROL NUCLEAR REACTIONS. THE U.S. NAVY'S NAUTILUS WAS THE FIRST NUCLEAR-POWERED SUBMARINE. THE NUCLEAR POWER ALLOWED THE SUBMARINES TO STAY AT SEA LONGER WITHOUT NEEDING TO REFUEL. OLDER SUBMARINES COULD ONLY STAY UNDER WATER FOR A FEW DAYS AT MOST. NUCLEAR SUBMARINES CAN STAY UNDER WATER LONG ENOUGH TO SAIL AROUND THE WORLD DOZENS OF TIMES.

IN 1997, THE UNITED STATES LAUNCHED THE CASSINI SPACECRAFT TO SATURN. THE MACHINE USED A SPECIAL ENGINE POWERED BY **PLUTONIUM**. LIKE URANIUM, IT PROVIDES NUCLEAR ENERGY. IT TAKES FAR LESS PLUTONIUM TO POWER A ROCKET THAN ROCKET FUEL.

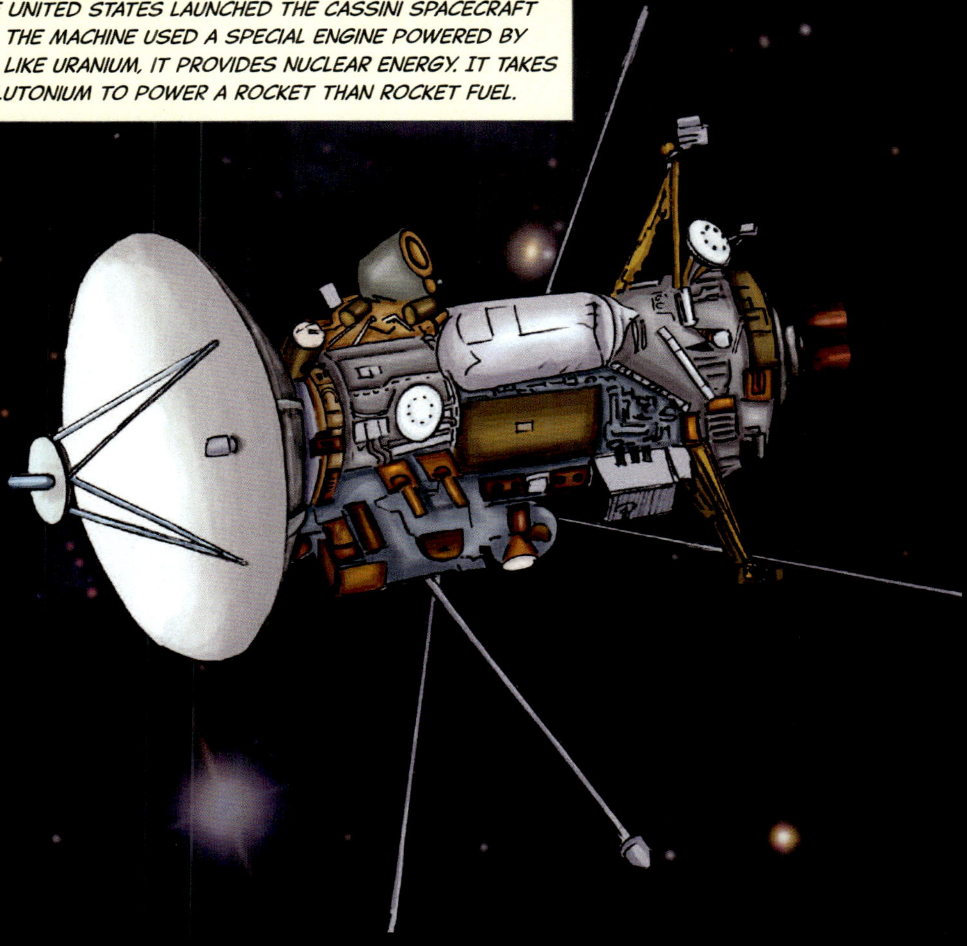

POWERING INTO THE FUTURE

TRAINS USED TO BE LUMBERING GIANTS. A FEW COUNTRIES ARE NOW USING FAST MAGLEV TRAINS. MAGLEV IS SHORT FOR MAGNETIC LEVITATION. USING THE POWER OF **ELECTROMAGNETS**, THE TRAINS FLOAT OVER A TRACK. MAGLEV TRAINS TRAVEL UP TO 310 MILES PER HOUR (499 KM/H).

THE REVOLUTION CONTINUES

TIMELINE

1690 – FRENCH SCIENTIST DENIS PAPIN DEVELOPS THE FIRST STEAM ENGINE.

1769 – JAMES WATT FILES FOR A PATENT FOR HIS STEAM ENGINE.

1783 – THE WORLD'S FIRST STEAMBOAT MAKES ITS DEBUT IN FRANCE.

1787 – JOHN FITCH INTRODUCES THE FIRST AMERICAN STEAM BOAT ON THE DELAWARE RIVER NEAR PHILADELPHIA, AS THE DELEGATES TO THE CONSTITUTIONAL CONVENTION LOOK ON.

1804 – RICHARD TREVITHICK BUILDS THE WORLD'S FIRST STEAM LOCOMOTIVE.

1807 – ROBERT FULTON'S FIRST STEAMBOAT, THE CLERMONT, SETS SAIL ON THE HUDSON RIVER FROM NEW YORK CITY TO ALBANY.

1814 – FULTON BEGINS REGULAR STEAMBOAT SERVICE ON THE MISSISSIPPI RIVER.

1869 – THE TRANSCONTINENTAL RAILROAD IS COMPLETED.

1885 – GOTTLIEB DAIMLER INVENTS THE WORLD'S FIRST MOTORCYCLE.

1885 – KARL BENZ BUILDS THE WORLD'S FIRST GASOLINE-POWERED AUTOMOBILE.

1903 – THE WRIGHT BROTHERS' FIRST AIRPLANE TAKES OFF AT KITTY HAWK, NORTH CAROLINA.

1913 – HENRY FORD PUTS THE FIRST ASSEMBLY LINE TO USE.

1945 – THE WORLD'S FIRST ATOMIC BOMB EXPLODES.

1947 – CHUCK YEAGER BECOMES THE FIRST HUMAN TO FLY FASTER THAN THE SPEED OF SOUND.

1954 – THE WORLD'S FIRST NUCLEAR-POWERED SUBMARINE, THE NAUTILUS, SETS SAIL.

1960S – JAPAN BUILDS ITS FIRST MAGLEV TRAIN LINE.

1969 – APOLLO 11 BLASTS OFF FOR THE MOON.

1981 – THE COLUMBIA BECOMES THE FIRST SPACE SHUTTLE TO ORBIT EARTH.

1997 – NASA LAUNCHES CASSINI PROBE TO SATURN.

GLOSSARY

ASSEMBLY LINE A METHOD OF MASS PRODUCTION DURING WHICH A PRODUCT, SUCH AS AN AUTOMOBILE, IS BUILT STEP BY STEP BY DIFFERENT WORKERS ADDING ONE PART AT A TIME

BOILERS A VESSEL THAT CONVERTS WATER INTO STEAM WHICH DRIVE ELECTRICAL GENERATORS

ELECTROMAGNET A TYPE OF MAGNET IN WHICH AN ELECTRICAL CURRENT PRODUCES A MAGNETIC FIELD

ENGINEER A PERSON WHO USES SCIENCE TO DESIGN MACHINES, ROADS, RAILWAYS, BRIDGES, SHIPS, AND OTHER THINGS

FREIGHT GOODS CARRIED BY A VESSEL OR A VEHICLE

GENERATE TO PRODUCE; TO CREATE

IMMIGRANT A PERSON WHO LEAVES ONE'S OWN COUNTRY TO SETTLE IN A NEW PLACE

JET A TYPE OF AIRPLANE THAT MOVES RAPIDLY THROUGH AIR IN ONE DIRECTION, PROPELLED BY A STREAM OF GASES MOVING IN THE OTHER

MECHANICAL ENERGY THE ENERGY OF AN OBJECT DUE TO ITS MOTION

NUCLEAR POWER ENERGY THAT COMES FROM A NUCLEAR REACTION

NUCLEAR REACTION CHANGES INVOLVING ATOMS

PATENT A DOCUMENT THAT PREVENTS OTHER PEOPLE FROM COPYING AN INVENTOR'S IDEA FOR A CERTAIN PERIOD OF TIME

PLUTONIUM AN ELEMENT USED IN NUCLEAR MATERIAL

POTENTIAL ENERGY STORED ENERGY; POTENTIAL ENERGY CAN BE RELEASED AND CONVERTED INTO OTHER TYPES OF ENERGY

INDEX

WEBFINDER

HTTP://WWW.THEHENRYFORD.ORG/EXHIBITS/HF/

HTTP://XROADS.VIRGINIA.EDU/~HYPER/DETOC/TRANSPORT/FULTON.HTML

HTTP://WWW.AECL.CA/KIDSZONE/ATOMICENERGY/NUCLEAR/INDEX.ASP

HTTP://WWW.GRC.NASA.GOV/WWW/WRIGHT/INDEX.HTM

HTTP://WWW.MOLLER.COM/